Blazers

The Best of the Best

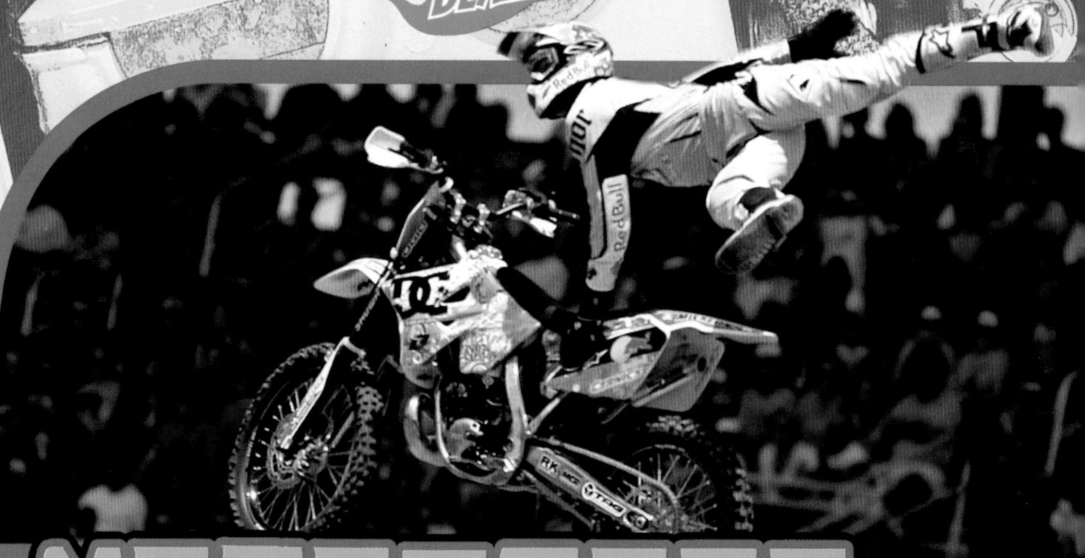

MOTOCROSS GREATS

BY LORI POLYDOROS

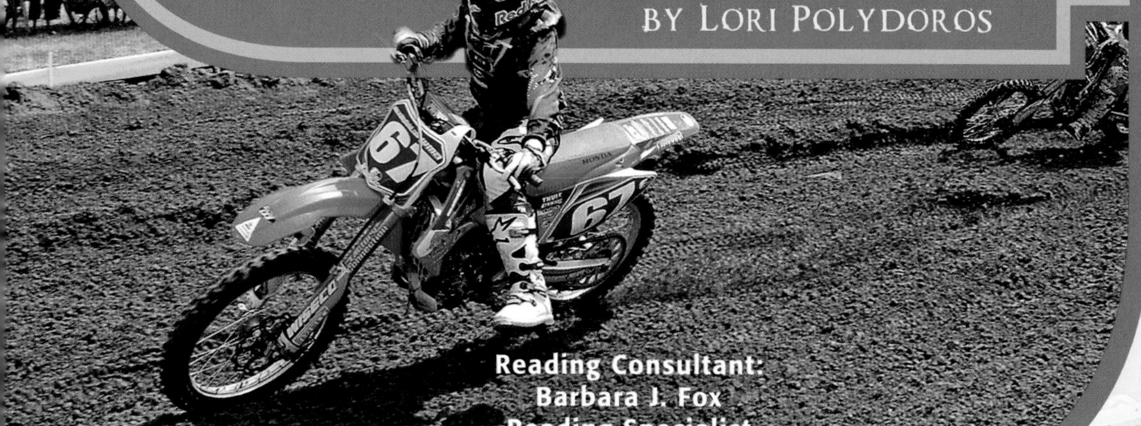

Reading Consultant:
Barbara J. Fox
Reading Specialist
North Carolina State University

CAPSTONE PRESS
a capstone imprint

Blazers is published by Capstone Press,
151 Good Counsel Drive, P.O. Box 669, Mankato, Minnesota 56002.
www.capstonepub.com

 Books published by Capstone Press are manufactured with paper
containing at least 10 percent post-consumer waste.

Library of Congress Cataloging-in-Publication Data
Polydoros, Lori, 1968–
    Motocross greats / by Lori Polydoros.
    p. cm.—(Blazers. Best of the best)
    Includes bibliographical references and index.
    Summary: "Lists and describes top motocross riders of the past and today"—Provided by
publisher.
    ISBN 978-1-4296-6499-8 (library binding)
    ISBN 978-1-4296-7249-8 (paperback)
    1. Motorcyclists—Biography—Juvenile literature. 2. Motocross—Biography—Juvenile
literature. I. Title.
GV1060.2.A1P65 2012
796.75092—dc22
[B]   2011002471

Editorial Credits

Mandy Robbins, editor; Kyle Grenz, designer; Eric Manske, production specialist

Photo Credits

AP Images: Reed Saxon, cover (top), Ric Francis, 1(top); Getty Images Inc.: Christian Pondella,
26-27, Jeff Kardas, 18-19, Stephen Dunn, 8-9, WireImage/Jamie Mullen, 6-7, 12; ISC Archives
via Getty Images/RacingOne, 28; Shutterstock: Warren Price Photography, cover (bottom),
1(bottom), 16-17; Steve Bruhn, 4-5, 10-11, 14-15, 20-21, 22-23, 24-25

Artistic Effects

Shutterstock: Warren Price Photography

Printed in the United States of America in Stevens Point, Wisconsin.
032011   006111WZF11

TABLE OF CONTENTS

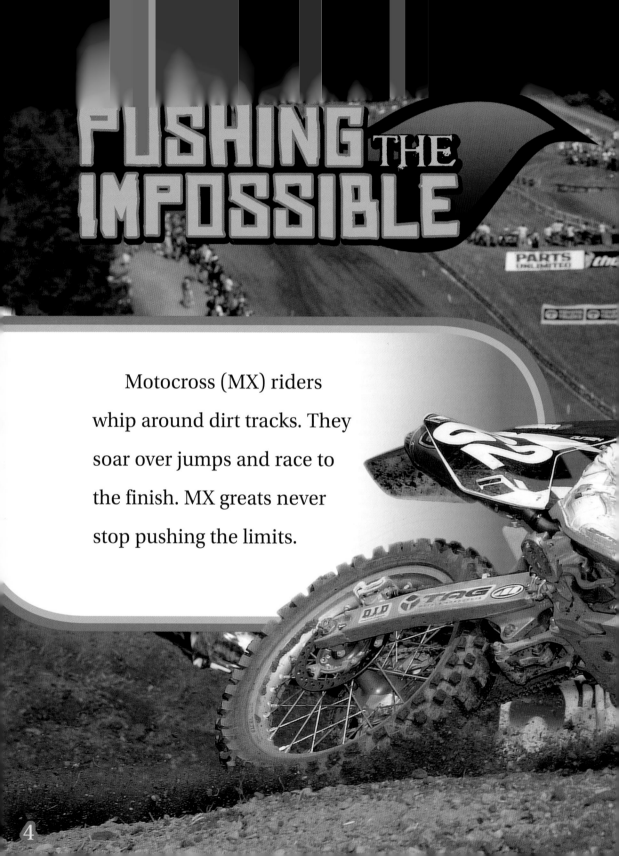

PUSHING THE IMPOSSIBLE

Motocross (MX) riders whip around dirt tracks. They soar over jumps and race to the finish. MX greats never stop pushing the limits.

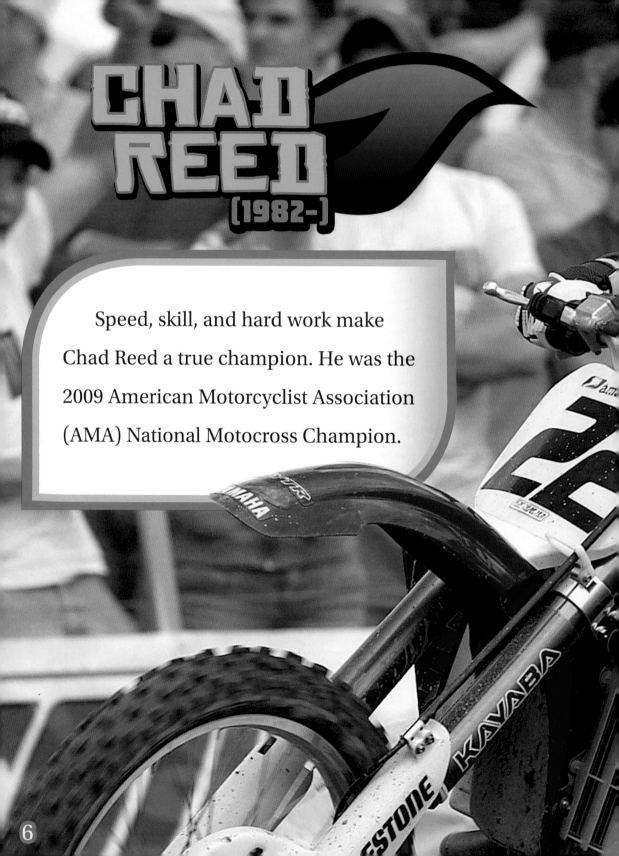

CHAD REED

(1982-)

Speed, skill, and hard work make Chad Reed a true champion. He was the 2009 American Motorcyclist Association (AMA) National Motocross Champion.

FACT Chad started racing motorcycles at age 4.

TRAVIS PASTRANA

(1983-)

Travis Pastrana won the AMA **Rookie** of the Year award in 2000. He has won almost every **freestyle** MX title there is.

FACT Travis is a multi-sport racer. He started racing rally cars in 2003. In 2011 he became a stock car racer.

rookie–an athlete who is in his or her first season as a professional

freestyle–a motocross style that includes jumps and tricks done in midair

JEFF EMIG
(1970-)

FACT Jeff holds 37 AMA national wins.

Jeff Emig makes MX look easy. He is a four-time AMA champion. Jeff has represented the United States in the **Motocross of Nations** six times.

Motocross of Nations—an annual motocross race where teams of three riders represent countries from all over the world

RICKY CARMICHAEL (1979-)

Ricky Carmichael's nickname is G.O.A.T. It stands for "Greatest of All Time." Ricky has won 16 AMA championships. In 2002 and 2004, he had perfect **undefeated** seasons.

 **FACT** Ricky quit MX in 2007 to race in the NASCAR Camping World Truck Series.

undefeated–having won every competition

RYAN VILLOPOTO
(1988-)

Ryan Villopoto has matched some of Ricky Carmichael's achievements. Both men won their first 450-**class** race. Each man has also won three 250-class titles in a row.

class—a division of racing; AMA pro races have two classes based on engine size—250cc and 450cc

FACT Ryan was a stand-out rider at the Motocross of Nations in 2007 and 2008.

JAMES STEWART

(1985-)

James "Bubba" Stewart is the first African-American to become a MX star. He was named Rookie of the Year in 2002. James was the 2007 AMA **Supercross** (SX) Champion.

FACT In 2008 James had a perfect MX season.

supercross–a type of motorcycle race held on a dirt track in a stadium

JEREMY McGRATH

(1971-)

Jeremy McGrath drew huge crowds to MX events in the 1990s. The **nac-nac** is his **signature trick**. Jeremy joined the Motorcycle Hall of Fame in 2003.

signature trick–a move that an MX rider is known for

TRICKED OUT!

NAC-NAC
a freestyle trick in which a rider appears to dismount his motorcycle in midair

FACT Kevin was the AMA Motocross Rookie of the Year in 1994.

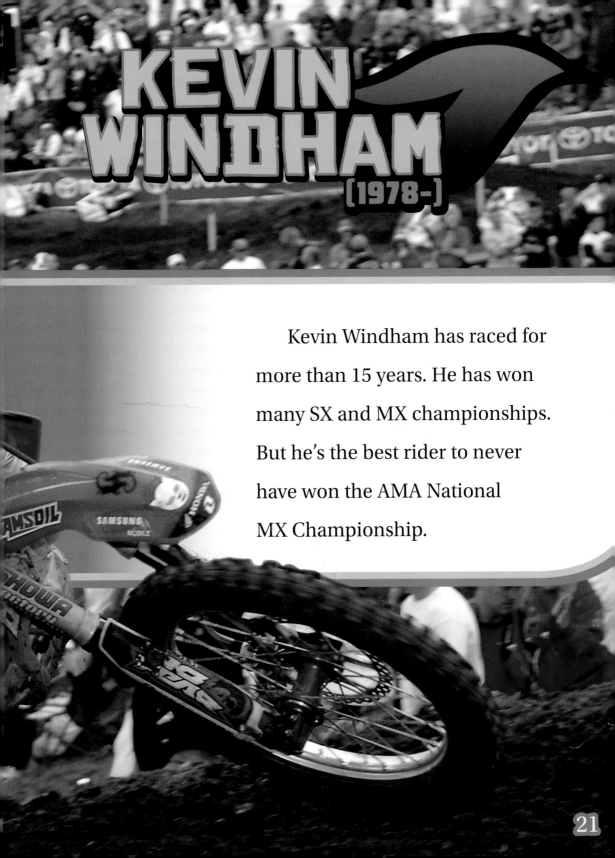

KEVIN WINDHAM

(1978-)

Kevin Windham has raced for more than 15 years. He has won many SX and MX championships. But he's the best rider to never have won the AMA National MX Championship.

Ryan Dungey is a rising MX star. He went pro in 2006, when he was only 16 years old. In 2010 he won AMA championships in both MX and SX.

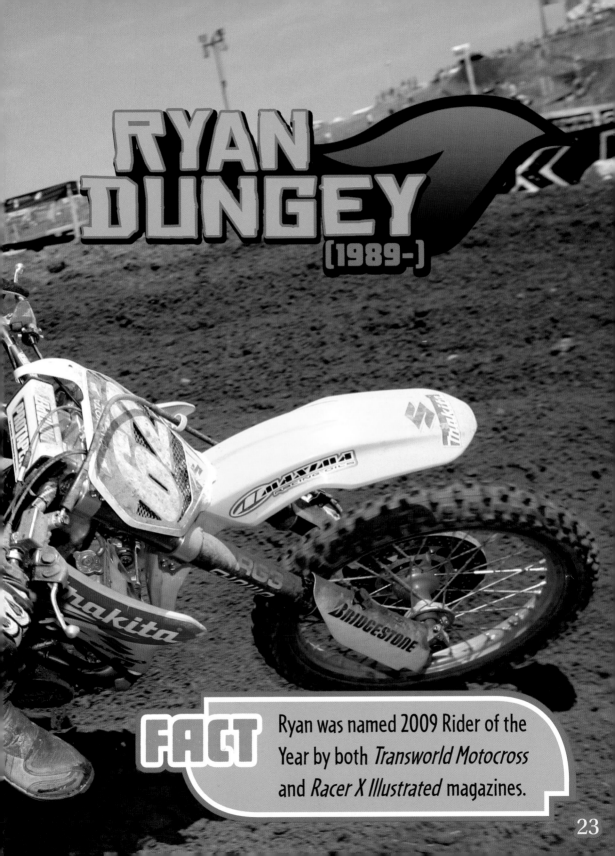

RYAN DUNGEY

(1989-)

FACT Ryan was named 2009 Rider of the Year by both *Transworld Motocross* and *Racer X Illustrated* magazines.

JESSICA PATTERSON

(1983-)

Jessica Patterson is the fastest woman in MX. She holds a **record** five AMA/Women's Motocross Association (WMA) championship titles.

record—when something is done better than anyone has ever done it before

ASHLEY FIOLEK

(1990-)

Ashley Fiolek is a two-time AMA/WMA champion. At 18 years old, she was the youngest rider to win a WMA championship.

FACT Ashley is the first deaf person to win an AMA national championship.

BOB HANNAH (1956-)

Bob "Hurricane" Hannah was a MX star in the 1970s and 1980s. He won seven AMA national championships. Like Bob, today's MX greats continue to push the limits.

FACT Bob trained in the desert instead of on tracks to sharpen his reactions.

GLOSSARY

class (CLASS)—a division of racing; AMA pro races have two classes based on engine size

freestyle (FREE-styl)—a motocross style that includes jumps and tricks done in midair

Motocross of Nations (MOH-toh-kross uv NAY-shuns)—a motocross race where teams of three riders represent countries from all over the world

record (REK-urd)—when something is done better than anyone has ever done it before

rookie (RUK-ee)—an athlete who is in his or her first season as a professional

signature trick (SIG-nuh-chur TRIK)—a move that a freestyle MX rider is known for

supercross (SOO-puhr-kross)—motorcyle races held on dirt tracks in indoor stadiums

undefeated (uhn-dih-FEET-ed)—having won every competition

READ MORE

Adamson, Thomas K. *Motocross Racing.* Dirt Bike World. Mankato, Minn.: Capstone Press, 2011.

Polydoros, Lori. *Awesome Freestyle Motocross Tricks and Stunts.* Big Air. Mankato, Minn.: Capstone Press, 2011.

Savage, Jeff. *James Stewart.* Amazing Athletes. Minneapolis, Minn.: Lerner Publications, 2008.

INTERNET SITES

FactHound offers a safe, fun way to find Internet sites related to this book. All of the sites on FactHound have been researched by our staff.

Here's all you do:

Visit *www.facthound.com*

Type in this code: 9781429664998

INDEX